LET'S READ A
BOOK

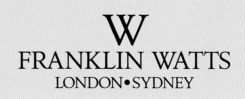

WRITTEN & ILLUSTRATED BY
RUTH WALTON

W
FRANKLIN WATTS
LONDON•SYDNEY

Do you like reading books?

The great thing about books is that you can read them just about anywhere!

You can read outside, inside, on the sofa, in the park, on the train, in bed or even on a plane.

Where is your favourite place to read?

When you want to read a new book,
it's good to go to the library.

The librarians sort the books out so that it
is easy to find the kind of book you want.

FICTION

The **fiction** section is
full of story books,
arranged by the name
of the **author.**

ALL ABOUT RABBITS

There are hundreds of different books in every library so you can always find something exciting to read!

Librarian

Fact books are kept in the **non-fiction** section, so if you want to find out about something, this is a good place to look. Non-fiction books are arranged by subject.

NON-FICTION

CRAFT

COOKERY

SCIENCE

GEOGRAPHY

ANIMALS

What is your favourite book?

All over the world, people love to read books. This book is written in the English **language,** but in different places people speak other languages and use different **scripts** to write them.

How many different scripts can you see?

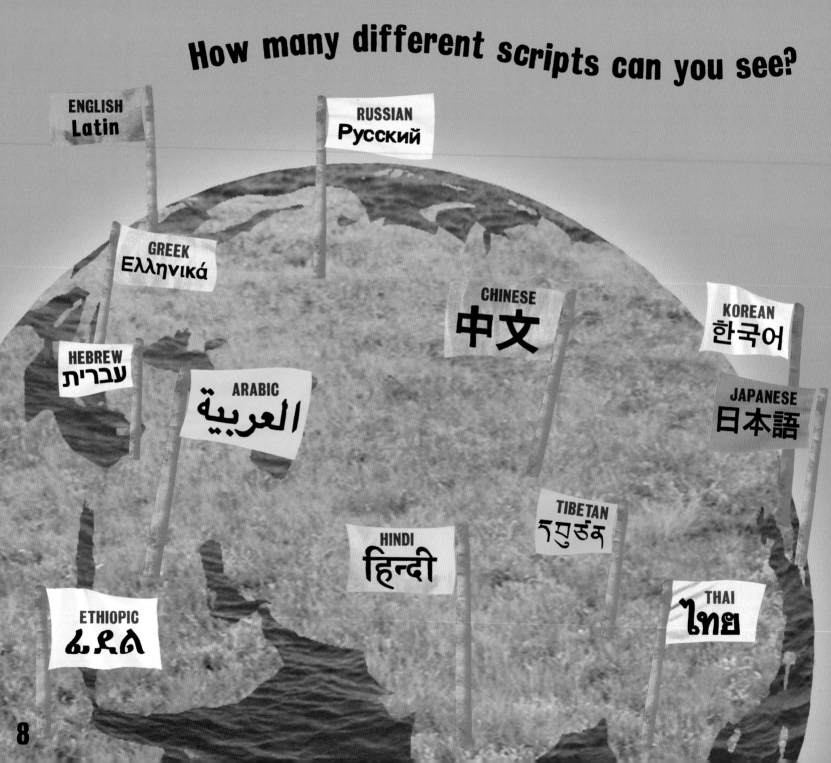

ENGLISH
Latin

RUSSIAN
Русский

GREEK
Ελληνικά

CHINESE
中文

KOREAN
한국어

HEBREW
עברית

ARABIC
العربية

JAPANESE
日本語

HINDI
हिन्दी

TIBETAN
དབུས

THAI
ไทย

ETHIOPIC
ፊደል

Braille is a kind of writing used by blind and **visually impaired** people. It was invented in 1824 by Louis Braille, who was himself blind, when he was only 15! The letters are made of dots, which are raised up so that people can feel them with their fingertips.

a	b	c	d	e	f	g	h	i	j

k	l	m	n	o	p	q	r	s	t

u	v	w	x	y	z

Try writing your name using Braille symbols!

The script that the English language is written in is called **Latin**. There are many more scripts that people use in different **cultures** around the world. In the past people used different scripts too.

When do you think writing was invented?

BOOKS and WRITING TIMELINE

3000 BCE

The oldest writing known to humans is called **cuneiform**, and was written by pressing sticks into wet clay. It was used by the **Sumerian** people.

3000-2000 BCE

Ancient Egyptians had three systems of writing called hieroglyphics, hieratics and demotic. They were usually written onto **papyrus**.

1500 BCE

In China, writing was scratched onto bones and shells. The first books were made out of **bamboo** strips. This ancient writing is still in use and has hardly changed.

900 BCE

The people of ancient Greece often wrote on pottery. Many of the letters in their alphabet are still in use today.

100 CE

The **Romans** wrote onto thin slices of wood or **scrolls** using the Latin alphabet.

500 CE

The first books were hand-written on **parchment**, and sewn together with string.

1400 CE

The **printing press** was invented and books became widely available for the first time ever!

How are books made now?

The person who writes the book is called the author.
If the book needs pictures they are made by an
illustrator or a **photographer**.

The photographer uses a camera.

An illustrator might use any of these things to make a picture.

How do you think the pictures in this book were made?

A **designer** arranges the words and pictures and shows the **editor,** who checks everything carefully to make sure there are no mistakes and makes an **index** for non-fiction books.

The designer uses a computer to arrange the words and pictures until they look just right!

The **publisher** arranges for the finished design to be printed on paper or made into an **e-book.**

Do you know what *paper* is made from?

Most paper is made from trees, but it can be made from other **fibres** too, including **hemp**, straw and **cotton**.

It takes around ten years for the tree to grow big enough to be cut down.

Where do the trees grow?

*A lot of paper is made from trees grown in special **plantations**, but some is made from trees from old forests. Look out for paper which has come from **sustainable** sources. This means the trees come from plantations that have been well cared for, and will be replaced when they are cut down.*

The trees are cut down and the branches are removed.
The logs and branches are taken away by trucks.

A worker who cuts down trees is called a lumberjack.

Log

Lumberjack

The wood is taken to a **paper mill** and turned into **pulp**. This is sprayed onto a wire **mesh**. The sheet of pulp is squeezed in a **press** to get some of the water out.

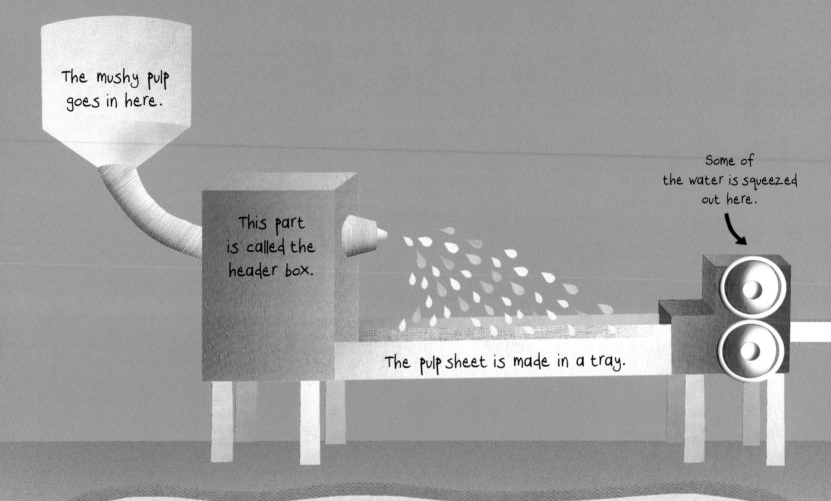

The mushy pulp goes in here.

This part is called the header box.

Some of the water is squeezed out here.

The pulp sheet is made in a tray.

How is pulp made?

*Some paper mills use **chemicals** to break the wood down into pulp, a mushy mixture of wood fibres and water. Others use machines to chop the wood into tiny pieces. Pulp can also be made from old paper, which is collected and mixed with water until it turns to mush. The ink is washed away using water and chemicals. In this way, paper can be **recycled** up to six times before the fibres get too small to use!*

The sheet of pulp has started to look like paper. It travels through heated rollers to help it dry out. The paper is smoothed and rolled onto reels that look like giant rolls of toilet paper!

Paper coating

Smoothing rollers

The pulp sheet is dried using heated rollers.

Some papers are coated in a special clay to make them look shiny.

The paper mill makes a lot of steam and smoke!

The paper is ready to be printed on.

At the **printer**, the roll of paper is loaded into the printing press. Inside the press it passes through lots of rollers.

Roll of paper

The paper travels through the press...

The rollers inside the printing press look like this.

Each roller has a **printing plate** on it that transfers the ink onto a special rubber sheet, which then transfers the ink onto the paper.

Each colour of ink has its own roller.

18

Lots of pages are printed onto one roll of paper. After the paper has been printed on, it passes over cold metal rollers which help the ink to dry. The prints are checked to make sure there are no mistakes!

This man is checking the printed pages.

... then the ink is dried inside here.

What is ink made from?

*Most printing ink is made from oil mixed with pigments. Oil is a material that formed under the Earth's surface millions of years ago from dead plants and animals. Pigments are dry colouring materials. Ink can also be made using other kinds of oil, including oil made from **soya beans**!*

How does colour printing work?

Most books are printed using only four colours of ink: black, yellow, cyan and magenta.

When the colours are printed on top of each other, they blend together to make different tones.

This is magenta.

This is yellow.

When magenta and cyan are printed on top of each other they make blue!

When yellow and magenta are printed on top of each other they make red!

When cyan and yellow are printed on top of each other they make green!

This is cyan.

This is the cyan plate...

This is the black plate...

This is the yellow plate...

The colours in the picture are separated, and made into individual printing plates.

When they are put together they make a full colour picture.

Here's the magenta plate...

...here are all the plates printed together!

Have you ever tried mixing paints to make new colours? What did you make?

21

How is the paper made into a book?

After the pages have been printed, they are **bound** together to turn them into a book. First the pages are **gathered** and folded using a machine.

This is the folding machine.

This is the stitching machine.

Next, the pages are stitched together and trimmed using a **guillotine.**

The pages are joined to the cover using glue.

When the glue has dried, the book is finished and ready to read!

Have a look and find out what the different parts of the book are called.

The cover of the book is made from **mill board.**

If you look at the centre of the pages of this book you can see the stitching that holds it together!

How many different scripts can you see?

All over the world people love to read books. This book is written in the English language, but in different places people speak other languages and use different scripts to write them.

ENGLISH
Latin

RUSSIAN
Русский

GREEK
Ελληνικά

HEBREW
עברית

ARABIC
العربية

CHINESE
中文

KOREAN
한국어

JAPANESE
日本語

HINDI
हिन्दी

TIBETAN
བོད་ཡིག

ETHIOPIC
ፊደል

THAI
ไทย

6

8

Braille is a kind of writing used by blind and visually impaired people. It was invented in 1824 by Louis Braille, when he was only 15! The letters are made of dots, which are raised up so that people can feel them with their fingertips!

Try writing your name using braille symbols!

The script that the English language is written in is called **latin**. There are many scripts that people use in different **cultures** around the world. In the past people used different scripts too.

When do you think writing was invented?

9

21

The pages of the book are numbered to help you find what you want.

The first and last pages of the book are called the **endpapers.**

The outer edge of the centre is called the spine.

What happens to the book next?

The books are packed into boxes and taken all around
the world to the places where they will be read.

SCHOOL

24

BOOKS
direct

Where could you find books in this picture?

THE CHEESE BOARD

EX LIBRIS BOOKSHOP

LIBRARY

25

Make your own book!

What you will need:

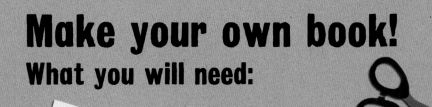

Pencil

Scissors

Small piece of card
(half a cereal box)

4 sheets of A4 paper
(used on one side)

Hole punch

30cm of string or ribbon

Step 2:

On the card, draw around one of
the folded pieces of paper twice, and
cut them out.

Punch two holes in the
short side of each piece
of card.

Step 1:

Fold a sheet of paper in half down
the longest side, so that any writing
is hidden inside!

Now fold it in half again.
Press the folds carefully.

Repeat with all four pieces.

26

Step 3:

Punch holes in the folded side of each piece of paper, and stack them all on top of each other.

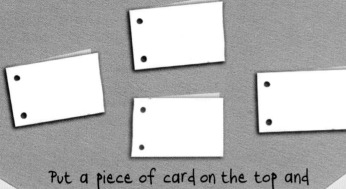

Put a piece of card on the top and bottom of the pile.

Step 4:

Line up the holes and carefully thread the string or ribbon into one and out of the other.

Step 5:

Tie the ends together with a double bow, just like you tie your shoelaces!

Your book is finished!

What are you going to write in it?

Glossary

Author the writer of a book, play or story

Bamboo a tropical grass plant that has hard woody stems

Bound tied or fastened together

Braille a kind of raised writing used by blind and visually impaired people

Chemical a substance produced by chemistry (the study of how things change when they are mixed together)

Cotton a natural fibre made from the seed pods of the cotton plant

Culture the language, customs, ideas and art of a particular group of people

Cuneiform an ancient kind of writing

Designer person who makes the design of a book

E-book a digital book

Editor person who reads and corrects pieces of writing, before they are published

Endpaper the first and last pages of a book, which are glued to the cover

Fibre a long thin part of a plant, animal or mineral

Fiction a made-up story

Gathered collected

Guillotine a machine for chopping

Hemp a fast-growing plant used to make paper or cloth

Illustrator a person who makes pictures for books

Index a list at the back of a book with page numbers showing where each thing on the list appears

Language a system of spoken and written words

Latin the alphabet and language of the ancient Romans. Their alphabet is still used today

Mesh a wire screen with small spaces

Mill board thick card

Non-fiction a book of facts

Paper mill a factory where paper is made

Papyrus a plant in Egypt that was used as a material to write on

Parchment a thin sheet of animal skin used for writing on

Photographer a person who takes photographs

Plantation an area of land used for growing crops

Printer a company whose business is the printing of books, newspapers or magazines

Printing plate thin sheet used in a printing press

Printing press a machine to transfer ink onto paper

Publisher a company that arranges for books to be made and sold

Pulp a soft wet material

Recycled processed to allow re-use

Romans the people of ancient Rome

Script the symbols used in writing

Scroll a roll of parchment

Soya beans beans from a soya plant

Sumerian people from the ancient culture of Sumer, now modern-day Iraq

Sustainable a way of managing resources so they will not run out

Visually impaired a person who cannot see very well, or not at all

Index

First published in 2010
by Franklin Watts

Text and illustrations
copyright © Ruth Walton 2010

Franklin Watts
338 Euston Road
London NW1 3BH

Franklin Watts Australia
Level 17/207 Kent Street
Sydney, NSW 2000

Series editor: Sarah Peutrill
Art director: Jonathan Hair
Photographs: Ruth Walton, unless
otherwise credited

Dewey number: 790.1'38
ISBN: 978 0 7496 8855 4
Printed in China

Franklin Watts is a division of
Hachette Children's Books, an
Hachette UK company.
www.hachette.co.uk